THE WORLDS OF ARCHITECTURAL DIGEST

CONTEMPORARY APARTMENTS

EDITED BY PAIGE RENSE

EDITOR-IN-CHIEF, ARCHITECTURAL DIGEST

THE KNAPP PRESS   PUBLISHERS   LOS ANGELES

Published in the United States of America in 1982
The Knapp Press
5900 Wilshire Boulevard, Los Angeles, California 90036
Copyright © 1982 by Knapp Communications Corporation
All rights reserved
First Edition

Distributed by The Viking Press
625 Madison Avenue, New York, New York 10022

Distributed simultaneously in Canada by Penguin Books Canada Limited

Library of Congress Cataloging in Publication Data
Main entry under title: Contemporary apartments.
(The Worlds of Architectural digest)
Selections from the pages of Architectural digest,
newly edited and designed.
1. Apartments. 2. Interior decoration.
I. Rense, Paige. II. Architectural digest. III. Series.
NK2195.A6C6   1982   747'.88314   82-8977
AACR2

ISBN 0-89535-104-8
Printed and bound in the United States of America

CONTENTS

FOREWORD

Many of the world's great cities are enjoying a lively renaissance today. Attracted by the diversity and excitement of the metropolis, more and more people of discernment are choosing to live in urban settings and consequently often in apartments. Because apartments seem to place more constraints on décor than houses, forward-looking designers must be both imaginative and practical. Most important, perhaps, they must welcome the opportunity to experiment, to invent.

The apartments selected from ARCHITECTURAL DIGEST for this volume are exceptional because their residents and designers have successfully created interiors rooted in a wholly contemporary idiom. And this has been accomplished without any sacrifice of style or comfort. Innovative, bold yet refined, freely but thoughtfully executed, these homes are as modern, sophisticated and dynamic as the cities of which they are a part.

At ARCHITECTURAL DIGEST we identify designs as "contemporary" when they emphatically express the present-day way of life. This is not to say they don't draw on traditional motifs or flourishes, or that all their furnishings and works of art were created within the past few years; it merely suggests that styles from the past do not predominate. Some of the qualities basic to contemporary design are sleek, simple lines; inventive use of lighting; subtle interplays of texture; and a well-ordered approach, in step with modern amenities and comforts.

As you might imagine, contemporary design frequently varies from city to city and country to country. That's why the contemporary apartments you'll encounter in

the following pages were chosen from around the world. These distinctive pent-
houses, pieds-à-terre, townhouses, lofts and apartments reveal the rich diversity of
contemporary design; all are unique, as are the talented people who created them.

As you become familiar with the designers included in CONTEMPORARY
APARTMENTS, I think you will be struck most of all, as I was, by the paradox of
their timeless quality. These interior designs, collectively, will stand as a tribute to the
past, a forecast of the future and, above all, a celebration of the present.

Paige Rense
Editor-in-Chief
Los Angeles, California

THE WORLDS OF ARCHITECTURAL DIGEST

CONTEMPORARY APARTMENTS

UNDERSTATED EASE

When people of a certain sensibility meet, background and language make little difference in communication. Deeper qualities of perception and instinct, though less definitive, are often more reliable. It was this kind of perception that came into play during a brief meeting between interior designer Sally Sirkin Lewis and a Japanese industrialist who needed a pied-à-terre in Los Angeles to use during business trips. His days in California would be busy, and he wanted a place to relax. After this first meeting, the remodeling of the condominium apartment was left to the designer's wit and talent. From his few words—"quality, contemporary, Western"—she projected a space of lush understatement with lacquer, stainless steel, raw silk, bleached and dyed oak floors and honey-colored leather. Although devoid of Oriental pieces at the resident's request, the space has a simple and restrained Japanese spirit.

"I set the pace simply, with understated ease," Mrs. Lewis says. "I developed colors based on the ones I love—camel, ivory, honey—all the colors I thought would be peaceful and easy. I picked leather, elegant and luscious, for the seating, because I couldn't visualize an excess of fabric. And I upholstered walls for soundproofing, silk everywhere but in the room used by his children when they visit, and guests." The apartment-turned-condominium was built in the 1950s, and it is typical of its time. Some rooms were small, underscaled and poorly spaced. The designer set about bringing everything up to contemporary expectations. Two bedrooms were made from three; bathrooms were gutted; certain windows were blocked off; closets were relocated.

Where the final achievement looks simple, it is rarely indicative of the work that went into it. In this case, restrictions beyond the ordinary created physical difficulties. For instance, because the building is concrete, nothing could be nailed to the walls. The molding, which is metal, had to be retained because of fire codes, and drains could not be rearranged. Finally, the tiny freight elevator that was to carry materials and workmen up and down eighteen flights could be used only during a certain few hours of the day. "It was a large project, an enormous undertaking," Mrs. Lewis says. "One perfect detail led to ten other perfect details. I hate the remodeled look, and I did such things as lining up a wall in one bedroom to make another space symmetrical. Another person might say, 'Who's going to notice?' My client noticed." Drapery tracks and pleats are recessed, hinges are hidden—all at no small effort. For example, because the door frames were larger than standard ones, hinges had to be modified to fit, then plated. Where metal or an improvement was needed—for air-conditioning vents, kitchen countertops and hinges—stainless steel now gleams.

The condominium apartment is characteristic of today, and what might have been arranged with bare minimalism by another designer takes on an international polish with its play of texture and surfaces. "I did not ask the owner about color or texture or fabric or finish," says the designer, "but when it came to what size bed he wished, if he wanted a shower or a tub, and where he wanted the stereo system controls, I contacted him in Japan. I learned a great deal about him." After the industrialist saw his residence and returned to Japan, he wrote Mrs. Lewis: "I would like to pay my respects to your high level of art, which has been fully reflected in the remodeling work of my home. I am amazed at the power of an interior designer to have turned an old apartment into such a beautiful place." More, then, than a design, the space illustrates two people's deep appreciation for each other's sensibilities.

A three-word description provided by her client—
"quality, contemporary, Western"— inspired
Sally Sirkin Lewis to conceive a design of understated ease for a sleek Los Angeles pied-à-terre.
PRECEDING PAGE: *In the Living Room, a group of
pre-Columbian figures seems to ponder ancient
riddles.* RIGHT: *Smooth monochromatic surfaces
create a sense of flowing expansiveness in the Living Room. Light-hued flooring of bleached oak
establishes an undulating pattern. Three* Vapor
Drawings, *by Larry Bell, shine with dark
iridescence; a soapstone sculpture,* Boy With
Leaves, *is by Zimbabwe artist Fanizani.*

Fletcher Benton's Painted Aluminum Blue Circle *charges the space around it with its structural boldness and vitality.*

In the Dining Area, a mirrored wall serves as a backdrop to an elaborate Ibo mask, while reflecting Gloria Kisch's mixed-media poles.

The Master Bedroom represents a textural medley, with silk bedcovering, velvet-upholstered sofa and chairs, and bedside chests of elm burl. The polished lacquered ceiling reflects the setting. A Bambara figure stands on top of a pedestal, and a mother-and-child sculpture from Zaire rests on the low table. The oil painting is by Sigrid Burton.

A FLAT IN GROSVENOR SQUARE

"Decoration is a matter of taking away, not adding," says Pandora Astor, and she follows this maxim with a second: "Never try to fit anything from one house into another." Heeding her own advice, she began designing her London flat in Grosvenor Square by selling all the furniture from her previous home. The next step was to eliminate things from the new flat: small fussy door frames; chair rails; pine alcoves. The pavement outside was no doubt chaotic, but the space inside was transformed. With new marble tiles on the floor, one vast expanse of white stretched from front to back, and Mrs. Astor was well pleased. "The rooms were just right then. I liked them even better when they were empty." She was, of course, understandably hesitant to sit on the floor forever, and added chairs with mock reluctance. "It is so very difficult to add things, because even the simplest object needs something else to balance it. What I can do without is more important to me than what goes with what."

There is a great deal that she does without very beautifully. Small tables, lamps, rugs—all represent clutter that she simply does not need or want. What she did want was substantial and comfortable furniture and a few fine objects. The objects she has chosen to include are carefully placed, and most of them have a sentimental value. A small gold cup was a gift from her godfather, the duke of Windsor; a wooden figure was bought by her grandmother from a church in Italy; the wicker basket that now holds wood was once filled with holiday delicacies.

Pandora Astor's love for cool white spaces is a legacy from a happy childhood in the tropics, where her father, Sir Bede Clifford, was a colonial governor. Silk draperies billow softly by an open window; a ceiling fan turns slowly in the kitchen; hurricane shades protect the candles. All this evokes thoughts of faraway places. Walls of dark mirror repeat the scene as though it were viewed through a filmy gauze, offering a mysterious glimpse of a different world. But these are not cold rooms, and it would be misleading to think of Mrs. Astor as too strict a purist in her love for white uncluttered spaces. She intends them as a comfortable background for the many friends who fill them: "People are not lost in a white room. What they are wearing alters it completely, and with walls, floors and ceiling the same color, they assume an importance in the space. Lighting, too, must be determined by how it affects the people in a room. It's the most important thing in decorating; overhead lights can make everyone look so unattractive. That's why I light the room with candles at night and dim the spotlights so they simply pick out a few things. Of course, the furniture must be arranged carefully to make it comfortable. The seating units were originally in an L-shaped arrangement, but I changed them after only one evening. We were all quite stiff-necked from trying to talk sideways."

Mrs. Astor is not a professional designer—although she has done a National Trust house—but her perfectionist approach and thoroughness might well be the envy of many professionals. She arranged to have all the marble tiles cut in Italy and imported, specifying that the graining must be straight—"not too squiggly and old-fashioned"—and then had it put down by a man from Malta, whom she describes as a "one-man-and-his-dog kind of craftsman." She notices details that would escape most eyes, even those of trained designers. These fine and gently colored rooms are tranquil, sharing a graceful refinement that has always been associated with Grosvenor Square. Some things, it seems, have not changed too greatly over the years and, as the old London music hall song so engagingly puts it: "It's delightful to breathe the air/Breathed by people in Grosvenor Square."

A tone of sleek modernity unifies Pandora Astor's design for her flat in Grosvenor Square, London. PRECEDING PAGE: *The English marble fireplace at one end of the Drawing Room is decorated in the elegant manner of Angelica Kauffmann.*

RIGHT: *A black mirror, reflecting the Drawing Room as through an Impressionist's veil, offers high contrast to the Italian marble flooring and to the pale fabric of sofas and draperies. The low wooden table was painted and lacquered to give the appearance of a granite surface. A marble torso adds a classical presence to the room.*

An early-19th-century Japanese screen is the
focus of the Dining Room. Its tones are echoed in
the Chippendale armchair nearby. Adorning the
travertine dining table is a 17th-century Italian
carved-wood figure that once belonged to Mrs.
Astor's grandmother; the hurricane lamps are
reminders of a childhood spent in the tropics.

In the Master Bedroom, an Italian dining table, used by Mrs. Astor as a dressing table, is accompanied by an amusing chrome adaptation of a tractor seat. Pale walls and fabrics contribute to the serene feeling of the décor. Doubly interlined draperies over blinds shield the room from the sometimes intrusive sounds of the city.

STYLED FOR TODAY

In certain Right Bank Beaux-Arts buildings in Paris, the experience of sitting in a living room in late afternoon is enhanced by a quality of fading pinkish daylight. This same lovely effect has been captured by interior designer Michael de Santis in a New York townhouse, where he admittedly set out to achieve a European flavor. He has achieved that flavor by a combination of rosy hues—from pale pink to deep maroon—and an architectural, rather than a decorative, use of mirrors, drawing light into the rooms. The residence is in a historic district in the East Sixties, and the area boasts some of the handsomest façades in Manhattan—including the 1870s townhouse whose interior Mr. de Santis has redesigned. There was no need, he felt, to make the usual clean sweep that tempts so many new owners of old houses. Certainly some structural changes were made to facilitate movement between rooms and to create additional facilities, but the preservation of the antique format is everywhere apparent: up the flights of an open staircase, with carpet and woodwork all in deepest rose tones, and in the diffused light coming from the original skylight that tops the stairwell—another continental touch.

This is no renovation, however, and it was the designer's good fortune not to be bound by even one previous possession. He built up the effect he desired by selecting the best contemporary American designs, as well as plush settees and sofas, and using that most luxurious of techniques, the upholstered wall. Although the colors are kept relatively close in value in most of the public rooms, there is a heavy emphasis on gently contrasting textures—raw silk and cut velvet—and these, in turn, are deftly played off against the sheen of lacquered furniture and the glint of glass. Both surface and color are combined in a liberal use of fine Italian marble.

To open a vista is a design concept in which Mr. de Santis excels, and he does it in entirely original terms. He expands views through glass and mirrors that force the observer to see space in a new way, and sometimes even beyond, in the infinity he creates with parallel reflections. The entrance hall of the home is a mirrored enclosure, but the view from it is an unobstructed one to the end of a burgeoning English garden. On the parlor, or second, floor, where entertaining took place in Victorian homes, the dining room is doubled by a mirrored wall. Elegant dinners become fairylands of candlelight, with the reflection of crystal candelabra and the glowing surface of a lacquered parchment table. A more traditional mirrored panel over the fireplace in the living room, extending up to the ceiling moldings, has arched niches on either side, with shelves to display a selection of glittering objects and small sculptures of crystal, gold and malachite. For every fireplace—each one retaining its Victorian marble mantel—there is a hand-carved glass fire screen. In transmitting the glow of firelight, the frosted glass spreads warmth and radiance into the rooms.

There is one more architectural *coup de force* Mr. de Santis has created, on the ground floor. The main feature of this room is a wall unit housing the most sophisticated electronic and computerized video-and-sound equipment. By night the room is alive with sound and light, and champagne glasses on open, illuminated glass shelves complete the design while proclaiming entertainment the purpose of this area. The champagne for those glasses comes from a cave below—a long, narrow room that serves as a wine cellar. The room is so long, in fact, that it extends under the street outside. New York City exacts fifteen dollars a year for this rare privilege, and the suggestions of an earlier era are inevitable.

The interiors designed by Michael de Santis for an 1870s New York townhouse evoke the sleek geometry and sensuous colors of Art Déco. PRECEDING PAGE: *A tall mirror, mounted on a raw-silk-upholstered Living Room wall, reflects the kindred lines of a lighted niche across the room.* RIGHT: *A mirrored fireplace wall visually enlarges the free-flowing space of the Living Room. Plump seating and a lacquered console continue the curvilinear mode. The painting is by Jules Olitski.*

ABOVE: *A hand-carved glass fire screen, one of several designed for the residence by Dennis Abbe, ensures the updated Art Déco effect.* OPPOSITE: *On a mirrored wall in the Dining Room is a narrow canvas by Jules Olitski. Silk drapery and upholstery fabric, and the parchment furniture finish, complement the deeper tone of the velvet wallcovering. Thoughtful lighting casts dramatic shadows.*

ABOVE: *In the Master Bedroom, a radiant focus is provided by a hand-carved glass fire screen. Traditional tailored draperies are outlined in the deeper tones of the crescent-patterned silk bedspread. A lacquered cabinet above the original Victorian marble mantel conceals a television set.*
OPPOSITE: *The Master Bath—a tour de force of versatility —includes a sitting area and dressing room. Rattan and mirror, outlined in bamboo, cover ceiling, closet doors and window shutters. The painting over the mantel is by Katja.*

ROMANCE OF BOHEMIA

Greenwich Village in the 1950s seemed an important place to be, if only because Abstract Expressionism, Beat poetry and Italian coffeehouses all centered there. However, the delinquent romance of Bleecker Street Bohemia has long since vanished, leaving behind a neighborhood rich not only in memories but also in the exceptional resources for living that were there long before the Village became the hub of the Beat Generation. Its lofts still provide some of the most luxurious living spaces in New York, a city where two of the most sought-after qualities are limitless space and a great deal of light.

Argentine-born painter Ronaldo de Juan's living-working loft was, when he found it, no more than an empty upper floor of a nineteenth-century warehouse. The chief advantages it had were ample dimensions and an exceptional feeling of openness. Rows of large windows on the south, west and north flood it with light by day and look out to the bright animation of the Village at night. Through Mr. de Juan's austere and sensitive approach, the interior has maintained its robust loft character while taking on an air of self-possessed and natural elegance. This is essentially a single space, with painting and living areas at one end and cooking and eating areas at the other. "And there is an enormous bathroom, because I love enormous bathrooms," states the artist. The original brick walls, the bare oak floors and the raw beamed ceilings have been left unchanged, and give texture and warmth to the vast open interior. The deliberately loose structure allows it to harmonize easily with the many moods of the artist's way of life. "I never had so much as the shadow of an idea of making a 'decorated' interior, Mr. de Juan says. "Let's say that the loft is simply conditioned to my way of living. It responds exactly to my interest in painting, books, music and cooking.

I basically feel that interior decoration in loft spaces is, more often than not, a catastrophe. Decoration tends to cover anything over in imitation materials, making it all a little like a movie set. Why should anyone want to bypass real materials, when real materials are so wonderful? A loft is not the place for *faux* malachite or any other annoying pretensions."

There are many souvenirs of his travels, like a lantern from Japan, and there are also "found" objects, such as the wooden horse discovered in the Bowery. He has also assembled a small but remarkable collection of ethnic sculptures. "I'm fascinated by pre-Columbian, African and Oceanic art. I don't want bibelots but *art*. It's very important to me, exactly like music. Music is a necessary part of my life, and there's every piece of sound equipment available here. For me, music is indispensable, like art and books and contact with the literary world. The other things that interest me are good food, and having marvelous friends." He entertains frequently, giving large dinners for artist friends such as Arman, Harold Stevenson and Leonora Carrington—"cultural dinners" cooked on a huge industrial stove, a present from his longtime friend Elaine, owner and impresario of the celebrated New York bistro for the literati, actors and café society.

But art is the central issue in Ronaldo de Juan's loft, and the interior is filled with the sweepingly turbulent rhythms and bold harmonies of his sometimes intensely colorful, and sometimes carefully subdued, canvases. The deceptively spontaneous look of the artist's compositions, with their self-possessed rhythms and their lyrical, profoundly poetic moods, are all expressions of a pure aesthetic vision and a restless imagination. They fill this open yet curiously intimate setting with an energetic sensuality and an engaging air of festivity.

*A loft in a 19th-century Greenwich Village warehouse, in
Manhattan, provides artist Ronaldo de Juan with ample
space and light.* PRECEDING PAGE: *The huge expanse, with its
original architectural features left exposed, is divided into
painting and living areas at one end, cooking and dining
areas at the other. At the center is a vibrant de Juan canvas.*

OPPOSITE: *A large New Guinea figure guards the Living Area.* ABOVE: *A sculpture collection includes several pre-Columbian, African and Baroque South American pieces, displayed on bookshelves and on top of a print cabinet. The drawing is a 1976 work by Mr. de Juan. An Argentine poncho adds color to the functional simplicity.*

LEFT AND ABOVE: *In the Dining Area, spot lighting focuses on a toy horse rearing from an Indian-cotton-draped table surface that is at times used as a buffet. The coffeepot and brass box are from a Marrakech street market; Mexican pottery and English bowls add harmonious touches of color and pattern. Wood and natural brick walls contribute warmth to the cavernous space. A floor was specially built with several layers of soundproofing material, sand and industrial oak.*

The Studio Area holds a number of
Ronaldo de Juan's large paintings and
his assortment of supplies. In the foreground, a Japanese lacquer-and-paper
lamp rests on a rectangular laminated-
plastic form that serves as a work surface. "Everything is useful, and every
object is put to use," says Mr. de Juan.

NEW YORK SIMPLICITY

The apartment that Jay Spectre completed for William Aucoin, in the Olympic Tower in New York City, is a paean to luxury and amenity. This is the Spectre style at its best: the skillful balance of décor, the use of peerless materials, and simplicity and honesty of design. "Actually there were many interesting things about this project," says Mr. Spectre. "First of all, there is seldom much to say about the buildings in New York—boring, bland and sometimes viewless. But the Olympic Tower is not only an exception to that rule, it also has a mystique of its own. I call it the *Normandie* syndrome. That French ship was a cynosure, the peak of 1930s design and decoration, and I feel that this apartment tower is the 1970s equivalent. It's certainly no coincidence that most of New York's leading interior designers have created at least one apartment in the building. Add to this the fact that we're dealing with higher-than-average ceilings and with a superb view, and you're almost bound to achieve a superior result."

But there is more than proportion or altitude at work here. There is an almost hypnotic sense of crisp and silky elegance in the apartment, seen most characteristically in the finishes of the living room. The east wall, clad in marble, reflects the glow of the view; the other walls and the ceiling are covered in a light-colored fabric, and the carpet is in the same tone. Plants and sculpture are the only elements not strictly tailored. It is as though the designer responded to the lyricism of the view with a commandment to himself: "Be controlled." Yet there is nothing arranged about these rooms. They are simply the unfolding of a response to luxuriance.

"I really see this apartment as a softening of my point of view. I feel that interior design is inexorably linked to the feeling of the times, to fashion, to all those movements that are in some way contingent upon the psychology of the moment. The hard edge, the abrupt line, of so much work of the 1970s now seems arbitrary—too much of an attempt to impose rules and force issues. Not that I think we're entering a sentimental period either, and I regard all talk of a Romantic revival as inappropriate. It's simply that extremism now appears too—extreme! First you prove a point, then you refine it, then you adapt it to a given situation. I guess you could say that's my general approach when I set about designing a room. Bill is an unusual young man, an entrepreneur in the music world, and he leads a very mobile life. I conceived of this apartment as comprising three key elements: the client, the space and myself. He let me have carte blanche, and I chose everything—fabrics, furniture, everything down to flatware and bed linens. I loved doing it. Which is not to say that this is my favorite way of working, much less my only way. But it is certainly a challenge. Bill Aucoin's way of life was what inspired me—even to the point of doing something that might seem a little excessive but was fun, such as mounting his gold and platinum records in the music room."

Actually, what the designer describes as "the music room" is a media center with highly sophisticated equipment. It displays another side of the designer's sensibility: his fascination with the finely engineered surfaces of modern life. "Those brushed stainless-steel panels in the living room are only masks to cover the heating and cooling systems, but to my mind they're the most exciting pieces of design in the whole space. It's a great challenge to create objects that function both on the technological level and as pieces of refined and pleasurable design." This observation might be applied to all of Jay Spectre's work, and particularly to this mixture of grandeur and modesty high above Fifth Avenue.

William Aucoin gave Jay Spectre carte blanche in the design of his Olympic Tower apartment, in Manhattan. PRECEDING PAGE: *The Entrance Hall announces the subtle neutral theme. To the right of the living room doorway is a painting by David Smith. Pre-Columbian sculptures adorn corner shelves.* RIGHT: *A breathtaking panorama endows the Living Room with a vivid sense of place. Sofas and armless chairs are flexibly placed on the diagonal. A sculpture by John Matt is mounted on a marble wall. Mr. Spectre designed the brushed-steel panels that mask air vents.*

BELOW: *In the Living Room, a bold painting by Robert Motherwell and a gleaming sculpture by John Matt are effectively paired. A sweeping expanse of windows reveals the city scene.*

OPPOSITE: *Subdued reflective surfaces surround a table set for dining. Seen in reflection is the painting by Robert Motherwell. The table and 19th-century Chinese chairs are covered in the same fabric that is used as wallcovering. The sculpture on the mirrored console is by Herbert Ferber.*

In the Master Bedroom, the spare
geometry of the design harmonizes with
the monolithic skyscrapers beyond. A
mirrored wall reflects upholstered cabinets and an 18th-century samurai suit
of armor. Above the bed is a painting by
Robert Motherwell, while the zigzag
steel sculpture is by Jeffrey Maron.

FOCUS ON ANTIQUES

The French château-style building in Beverly Hills was not antiques dealer Rose Tarlow's idea of good architecture. However, basically she liked the apartment she chose. Since she divides her life between California and London, she needed something in Beverly Hills she could lock up and leave. So, with customary candor, she set about making the most of the apartment by stripping away the plaster roses and gingerbread that are characteristic of much southern California architecture of the 1930s.

Design in the apartment is kept to a minimum. "I love antiques, but I don't think they should be overpowering in a building that doesn't have any real architectural interest," says Mrs. Tarlow. "Some of the designers I admire and have learned from—Syrie Maugham, Rose Cumming, Jean-Michel Frank, Billy Baldwin—all have said, in their own ways, that interior design is best when it is in keeping with the architecture. *Suitability* was Elsie de Wolfe's main word in the area of design." Mrs. Tarlow was determined not to give in to the temptation of using too many antiques. Rooms are kept to one color; floors, walls, windows, slipcovers and woodwork are all in the no-color tones of sand and wheat fields and willow baskets. With the exception of the bedroom, one fabric is used throughout—a poplin that Mrs. Tarlow describes as "like some raincoat material."

"These rooms are carefully plotted and planned, decorated and thought out," she says. "Rooms I've had in the past tended to be soft and rambling, with a feeling that they'd been there forever, but that effect would have looked foolish in this apartment." Thus, a number of her favorite antiques were sent to her London apartment. "I lead a different kind of life there; I don't go out much. The weather is cold, and I have a fire going and people in. In California I'm up very early in the morning, out riding my horses in Malibu, where I also spend weekends. During the week I'm at my shop, and when I get home in the evenings I don't want to look at *things*.

"But, you know, I do love objects. I grew up around antiques, and there are times when I'd rather read about antiques than read a novel. I've given lectures on antique furniture, and I think anyone who wants to know about pieces should first know the periods, find out what was going on in different countries during a given era. Once you know the history, the furniture falls into place." Thus, objects play only one part in her design. "I don't get attached to pieces as much as I do to the feeling of a whole room." If suitability is the first requirement for good design, then the often illusive quality of pleasure is the second. "To walk into a room and be happy you're there seems very important to me. What else is there, really? I've been in rooms that have that feeling, and I think people will never be tired of living in them. This feeling comes from many things—the time of day, the light, from being truthful in what you design. There is no point in doing something merely for an effect, or because you're worried about what other people may think. The feeling of contentment also comes from a room where everything is crisp and clean, where the furniture is polished and the floors shine."

An understanding of quality and design comes through experience. "I believe that anything good will fit into any environment. Perhaps that's where interior designers and antiques dealers part company. Many designers will use a piece only if it fits into a room; to an antiques dealer, the object comes first and will be used whether it belongs or not. Often, of course, this leads to clutter. I've tried to eliminate that from this apartment, and it's ten times harder to be very strict with yourself."

PRECEDING PAGE: *Each element in the Living Room reinforces Rose Tarlow's unified design for her Beverly Hills apartment. A single light hue introduces a sense of purity, which is enhanced by informal slipcovered furniture. Simple, distinctive forms assume added importance within this disciplined décor. Nineteenth-century Japanese bronze candlesticks and an American Indian basket adorn the 17th-century French stone chimneypiece.* RIGHT: *A Louis XV fauteuil, upholstered in leather, complements a 17th-century Flemish table and mirror in the Living Room.*

OPPOSITE: *The Dining Room perpetuates the mood of candid simplicity pervading the apartment. Carefully integrated antiques include a Chinese table bearing an American weather vane, 19th-century Japanese lacquered candlesticks and, silhouetted against a Japanese screen, a collection of Roman flacons. The reclining stone figure of a woman is by Jacqueline Bez.* ABOVE: *In the Kitchen, a dark granite counter contrasts with the expanse of bleached-oak cabinetry. Introducing a rustic flavor are hemp matting, a French rope-covered armchair, and a child's ladderback chair.*

ABOVE: *In the Study, the linear emphasis established by wooden blinds and flooring sets off diverse rounded appointments: a French Régence fauteuil, an 18th-century Peruvian jar atop a Chinese stand, and a chaise longue upholstered in old leather. On the graceful goat-leg table, an antique celadon bowl from Korea holds parley with an antique French wooden bowl.* OPPOSITE: *In the Master Bedroom, a mist of French voile is a soft variation on the monochromatic theme.*

CORNUCOPIA IN SOHO

Of all the lofts in New York's SoHo, that of Ivan and Marilynn Karp perhaps tells more than any other about the tastes and preoccupations of the art community. Owner of the O. K. Harris Gallery, Ivan Karp has for over fifteen years exerted an incalculable influence on contemporary art and collecting. Both Mr. Karp and his wife, sculptor Marilynn Gelfman-Pereira, are themselves contagiously enthusiastic and avid collectors. One of the most important paintings of the Photo-Realist movement, Richard Estes's *Cafeteria,* is here, while an eighteenth-century marble bust signed *Houdon* occupies an adjacent niche. Flanking a robust paper-stock trolley—now in service as a table—two long leather sofas boast souvenir cushions from the New York World's Fair Hall of Transportation. On the other side of the vast room there is a display of nineteenth century American stoneware crocks with their sturdy, sparsely ornamented glazed bodies.

"The loft," says Marilynn Karp, "is really one large collection called 'things we think are wonderful objects'—and we look for them with passion." The only unifying factors are vitality and frequently an unassuming directness that Ivan Karp terms blunt. "American art," he says, "has taught us to be unself-conscious about admiring blunt objects. We are in a country of short traditions, with a focus of two centuries. Most of the elegant production has been plucked out, and the available areas for collecting have become exotic—and expensive. We follow our instincts for things that were not conceived of as decorative objects, but rather are articulate objects where materials are visible without disguise. We look for the blunt and the wholesome, things with good planning—elegance without 'high art.' "

With its superabundance of art and objects, the loft is without any gallery/museum undertones.

Much in the living area is oriented toward food, another field that holds limitless fascination for the Karps. And the immense studio is ordered around Marilynn Gelfman-Pereira's worktable, strewn with the twigs, bird bones, thorns and wires she uses in her constructions, mixing twentieth-century technology with aspects of craft tradition. "I have the ability to deal with small and petty objects until they build up to something meaningful," she explains. Art and objects nominated by the Karps as *art* are everywhere. There are paintings by the Pop artists Ivan Karp discovered and promoted, such as Andy Warhol and Roy Lichtenstein. There are works by the Photo-Realists he shows at his gallery: John Salt, Robert Cottingham, Robert Bechtle, Richard McLean, Ralph Goings, John Kacere and John Baeder. Most appealing is the feeling that each object has inherent qualities that are important and passionately appreciated by its owners.

The enthusiasm for which Ivan Karp is famous touches everything in the loft, a space he defines as "unplanned, instinctual and incongruous, the result of reacting to feelings, not information." Even the most humble chair can capture his imagination. "These are things you see everywhere, but they have vitality. They have history, nostalgia, patina. I have a flirtatious eye for objects, and these objects seduce me. They put me in a condition of unreasonableness. When I see one, I need it. How can I leave it in melancholy isolation in someone's shop?" Because artists, collectors and museums continually turn to Ivan Karp for his opinions of contemporary art, friends often call him to ask: "What are you buying now?" "Being a pioneer," he explains, "is a great satisfaction. But it's a question of being first, not 'What are you collecting now?' Collecting is an open admiration that perhaps leads to pioneering."

Gallery owner Ivan Karp and his wife, sculptor Marilynn Gelfman-Pereira, live in an art-filled SoHo loft, in New York City. PRECEDING PAGE: *Marilyn Levine's stoneware* Jacket *hangs, appropriately, in the Entrance Area with paintings, from left to right, by Porfirio Di Donna, John Clem Clarke and Ralph Goings.* ABOVE: *The Living Area features* Le Duc de Berry, *by an anonymous French artist, and Richard Estes's* Cafeteria. *Mounted on a track, the Estes painting slides upward to reveal a television set.*

In a corner of the Studio, John Chamberlain's metal sculpture looks strikingly modern amid a varied mise-en-scène that includes Peter Saari's contemporary Pompeiian Fresco and a classical head of the Roman emperor Balbinus. The American salt-glaze stoneware reflects Mr. Karp's appreciation for "things that were not conceived as decorative objects, but rather are articulate objects where materials are visible without disguise."

51

A series of portraits lends a venerable aura to
the Dining Area. Appointments include a 19th-
century harvest table and early-20th-century
chairs. An Art Nouveau figure in the corner,
a Chiparus dancer on the table and a bronze
Diana by Falguière add expressive animation.

The collection of antique portraits continues in the Library. Bookshelves display a friendly intermingling of books, salt-glaze stoneware and other objects both pleasing and unusual. Augmenting the bibliophilic atmosphere are an oak desk chair and an antique oak rolling ladder.

A grouping of contemporary paintings and drawings includes works by Richard McLean, Idelle Weber, Robert Cottingham, John Baeder, Richard Estes and Ralph Goings. Small Art Nouveau sculptures frolic on the cabinetry surface below. At left is a Victorian slot machine.

Nineteenth-century American and continental landscape paintings produce an air of tranquility in the Master Bedroom. The group of sculptures includes a Gaston Lachaise bronze. A delicate Art Déco stained glass door insert and a leaded-glass lampshade serve to diversify the mood.

PARISIAN TOUCH

Interior designers who are given carte blanche find they have the kind of freedom generally reserved for the painter and the sculptor. Under such circumstances, designers, free to experiment with forms and themes and colors, have a unique opportunity to create something with a personal stamp—to arrange the "ideal setting" that they rarely have the time or the occasion to realize. However, the temptation is then great to forget that interior design, unlike painting, is successful only when brought to life by the presence of the people who are destined to live with it. Faced with a minimal and almost nonexistent décor, Parisian interior designer Jacques Grange had the good sense not to abuse the privileges of total freedom. To justify the resident's confidence in him, he felt obliged to establish an unobtrusive décor that is not overwhelmed by furniture and objects, but is carefully thought out and structured.

First of all, he put to rights everything about this contemporary Parisian apartment that was banal and monotonous. He remodeled narrow window frames and pulled down partitions as well as adding a stairway, a fireplace and a terrace. Basically, he conceived an open design in the form of an L. As M. Grange explains, "I wanted to show that it is possible to arrange a fairly rigid space, based on the square and the right angle, without turning it into a sepulcher of metal and lacquer." The designer, in fact, has never particularly liked to use such materials, finding them cold and overly fragile. One particular trip to Italy—to Siena—provided him with the inspiration he needed for the present apartment. He returned to Paris with memories of the warm and versatile materials he had seen in Tuscany: the wood, the sand, the terra-cotta, the straw. These simple and natural substances are not often used extensively in a sophisticated residence, and perhaps only the Japanese have really considered them to be noble—noble enough to have decorated many of their palaces. "Such natural materials only improve with age and soon develop interesting patinas of their own," says M. Grange. In keeping with this concept, he has used straw window blinds that are reminiscent of Japanese rice-paper screens.

The interior of the apartment M. Grange has arranged is basically given over to two general areas: one devoted to hospitality and the other to private family life. The pivot that joins the two is the staircase itself, in the hands of the designer not simply a passageway but a sort of sculpture, a labyrinth of mirrors, with something of the unreal and imaginative feeling that is associated with the theater. Thanks also to his careful study of the work of Jean-Michel Frank, M. Grange has developed an approach that is concerned far more with the question of proportion than with any mere arrangement of objects and furniture. Frank's example taught him that discipline and simplicity need not produce a décor that is impoverished and graceless.

The lessons are very clear in the unassuming and fitting materials of this Paris apartment: the terracotta, the natural wood, the preference for furniture designs based on the cube and the square. Paradoxically, the general effect is one of extreme classicism. It is a classicism, however, that can accommodate many different styles: the Chinese ironwood chair in the entrance hall or the Greek-style chairs in the dining room. Above all, Jacques Grange has created a feeling of freedom. From one point of view, the designer has really been a sort of theater director. He has given careful attention to space and placement and the development of a design choreography. A set the apartment may be, but it is one ready and welcoming for its actors.

In his design for a Paris apartment, Jacques Grange achieved a refined balance of contemporary appointments, natural materials and superlative art and decorative objects. PRECEDING PAGE: *An 18th-century Chinese armchair provides an exotic note in the Entrance Hall, where mirrored surfaces create an illusionary labyrinth of staircases.* RIGHT: *The warm tones and textures of the Living Room are established by terra-cotta tiling, woven-straw window shades and suede upholstery. Wall niches display a 14th-century Greek amphora and an 18th-century sculpture of a woman.*

The earthy tones of the terra-cotta tiling and upholstery fabrics in the Living Room were inspired by the simple and natural materials the designer encountered on a trip to Italy. The painting is by Miró. Japanese lacquered chests, positioned at each end of the sofa, serve as tables.

Grids of sycamore punctuate the mirrored Dining Room walls and ceiling with rectilinear precision. The table, accompanied by Greek-style chairs, offers a genteel setting of antique glass and porcelain dinnerware. The richly inlaid commode in the background adds an exotic presence.

Sycamore strips, which were used as
effective accents in the entrance hall and
dining room, proliferate in the Master
Bedroom, where they provide an interesting textural contrast to the rest of the
décor. A pair of Matisse drawings
complement one by Léger, at right.

Augmented by mirrors and marble, the tone of graceful simplicity in the master suite culminates in the Master Bath, where a wall of sycamore curves to separate a whirlpool spa from the bedroom. Translucent window screens enhance the effect of airy purity.

THE URBAN FLAVOR

"People do not immediately identify this as a 'Michael Taylor' interior," says the San Francisco designer. "I take that as a compliment—to my client and to myself." Mr. Taylor is speaking of the three-story Park Avenue penthouse apartment he completed for its resident and his young son. "When I saw the apartment, I immediately knew the direction in which I wanted to go," he says. "My client not only agreed with the concept but saw what I saw, and then we went on to carry it all out with dispatch."

A wave of color and light carries through the apartment, and within that context Mr. Taylor allowed specific pieces of furniture and art to dictate the needs of various rooms. In the living room, four Régence-style chairs define that particular space, their classic simplicity suggesting the need for understatement in the room. A large Morris Louis canvas in the garden room is the basis for the design of that area. Rather than introduce other works of art into the room, the designer lined the walls with mirrors to reflect the Louis painting tenfold. An enclosed greenhouse separates the garden room from the dining room, inviting sunshine and greenery into the city apartment, quite as if it were a California beach house. The tremendous play of light is increased by uncovered windows, and at night the cityscape envelops the dramatic interiors.

Michael Taylor instills into interiors a marriage of sophisticated elegance and casual freshness that appears spontaneous. Such spontaneity, however, is one of the most difficult interior design effects to achieve. The ability to integrate the positive elements of various regions—the casual outdoor living of the West Coast, the candlelighted warmth of a New England winter and the elegance of a grand European household—is the result of careful observation and experimentation. "As a designer," says Mr. Taylor, "I am influenced by the location of the project with which I'm involved. This is a penthouse apartment on Park Avenue, surrounded by terraces that are over twenty floors above the street. The design direction was largely determined by the surroundings. I undertake projects everywhere in the world, and it is always intriguing to work in new environments, climates and cultures. These are the experiences that teach and train designers, and this is how we are inspired to produce fresh new ideas.

"For every interior there is a design solution. It is up to the designer to experiment until he finds the solution that works for his client and for himself, and the best solutions are those that appear to be the simplest to achieve. Critics often don't realize how many ideas are cast aside before a designer arrives at the most direct solution to the problem facing him. If there's one particular sentence to describe my work, it's 'When in doubt, take it out.' When I reach an impasse during a project, I eliminate—never add. If there's a question about the success of a given room, I take furniture out—and keep thinning it out until the design solution is the simplest it can be. This is, no doubt, contrary to the practice of many designers who, when in doubt, add another pattern, texture or piece of furniture, until a room is smothered. The result is arbitrarily defined as 'eclectic.'

"I find, however, that an eclectic interior does work well for people who have traveled widely and own beautiful things. I'm charmed by their desire to surround themselves with personal treasures to which memories and experiences are attached. This apartment, for example, includes many possessions, primarily antiques, from my client's previous home. But essential to the success of the apartment is the fact that the pieces are used artistically to achieve a clean and classic design that is very satisfying."

Michael Taylor fused simplicity with sophistication in a penthouse apartment on Park Avenue, in Manhattan. PRECEDING PAGE: *In the Living Room, Mr. Taylor's extensive use of travertine establishes thematic unity.*

RIGHT: *Like ripples sculpting a field of wheat, restrained furnishings create rhythmic currents amid the neutral tones of the Living Room. Four Régence-style fauteuils afford contrasting period accents. Dappling the ceiling with shadow, strategically placed islands of foliage inject flourishes of color.*

In the Garden Room, rills of color cascade down a painting by Morris Louis; Hugo Robus's sculpture Yearning *is reflected above the mantel. The table, a disk of polished granite, is surrounded by chairs suggesting snug containment. Snowy marble flooring adds hard-surface luster.*

FOLLOWING PAGES: *Dark glamour envelops the Master Bedroom, where the midnight tones of walls and carpeting suggest mysterious depths. Japanese soy tubs, serving as planters, pose a rustic contrast to the sophistication of the room.*

A ceiling of polished steel shimmeringly distorts the image of the Media Room, which is designed to accommodate film and television screenings. The painting, Future Perfect, *is by Lee Krasner, and the sculpture in silhouette atop the wedge-shaped table at the left is by Masyuki Nagare.*

ORIENTAL CALM

On the Left Bank of the Seine, in Saint-Germain-des-Prés, the collector and connoisseur Jean-Michel Beurdeley discovered an ideal residence for himself, his wife and their son. Located near the gallery he owns, which specializes in Far Eastern art, the apartment is also a flawless setting for his most prized personal pieces from the Orient. The family occupies the "parlor floor" of an old house, arranged for them by interior designer Edouard Salas. Since the original mantelpieces and boiseries had long since disappeared, the interior was renovated without doing damage to existing classical décor. Proportions were excellent, and, in fact, designer Eileen Gray, the previous resident, used these large rooms and high ceilings to great effect as a background for her own fine work in metal and lacquer.

Both M. Beurdeley and his interior designer wanted to use this generous and well-balanced space in the most compelling way possible. Indeed, Edouard Salas had received his early training as an architect, and he understood exactly what the owner had in mind: to show to best advantage those splendid objects M. Beurdeley finds each year on his voyages of exploration to the Far East. He chooses the pieces for their rarity, for their originality, but perhaps above all for their shape and color—elements that allow him to create appropriate and arresting ensembles. "It has always been my conviction," he says, "that objects in themselves create good décor." Edouard Salas, having returned the space to its original purity, sheathed the walls with simple wood and straw. In keeping with this understated approach, he set here and there on a neutral carpet a number of wooden pedestals, Japanese in inspiration. On these pedestals the Oriental objects receive the necessary focus and also provide important rhythms in a space that has been purposely simpli-

fied. Here are no golden Buddhas displayed against a mirrored background or standing in special niches. In contrast, an uncomplicated dialogue between objects of various Oriental origins has been created.

This sensitivity is understandable, since Jean-Michel Beurdeley studied, and came to appreciate, the Orient in a very special school. Early in life, his father, the historian Michel Beurdeley, taught him the meaning of China Trade porcelain as well as an understanding of taste in the Middle Kingdom itself. At a young age he enjoyed yearly trips to the Far East. Extensive knowledge, fortunately, has never dampened his aesthetic sense. For example, if he discovers a piece of sculpture he likes, he is far more interested in the modeling of the body than in its purely antiquarian aspects. "And I have no desire to fall into the trap of the specialist who thinks that everything rare is automatically beautiful."

In his apartment, too, there is no furniture that interferes with the harmony of objects, and even the Chinese armchairs—where no one ever sits—are considered in terms of sculpture. What furniture is there is discreet and functional: the smoked-glass table in the dining room; the classic designs of Mies van der Rohe; several low Japanese tables; and the bedroom, with vestiges of the décor created by Eileen Gray. As a matter of fact, operating on the principles of mobility found in the Japanese house, Jean-Michel Beurdeley likes to change objects constantly. For this purpose he keeps on hand a special reserve of favorite objects so that he can create apparently spontaneous compositions like those often found in the alcoves of Japanese teahouses. In so doing he maintains flexibility while nourishing a mood of Oriental repose. And the superlative objects he carries back from the Far East are completely at ease in the midst of the scintillating French capital.

Designer Edouard Salas devised a serene setting for Asian art in the Paris apartment of Jean-Michel Beurdeley. PRECEDING PAGE: *In the Living Room, a 17th-century Japanese screen depicts cavorting horses; to the right is a wooden monk in a reflective pose.* ABOVE: *An 8th-century Siamese Buddha, in the Living Room, embodies contemplative grace. Occupying the alcoves beyond are a pair of 17th-century Chinese cabinets.*

Straw-textured paper on a Living Room wall provides a subtle background for an 18th-century Chinese table and a balanced assemblage of art. A Tutundjian oil painting and a construction by Soto offer a modern contrast to Asian sculptures: a 9th-century Javanese head of Buddha, at left, and a Cham deity head from the 11th century.

Like a sweeping picture window, a pair of 17th-
century Japanese screens by Tsunenobu presents
a panoramic landscape in the Dining Room.
Bestowing tranquil dignity are an 11th-century
Buddha and 8th-century Cambodian figures—a
torso and, in the foreground, a statue of Vishnu.
The 17th-century Chinese temple table at the
right adds ornament and weight to the décor.

In the Master Bedroom, the modern spirit is represented artistically in a Tutundjian collage and a larger Marcelle Cahn painting—both created in 1925. A 9th-century Javanese carved stone deity head rests at bedside, while the bookshelves bear, from left to right, a 17th-century bronze head of Buddha, a 7th-century Chinese marble stele and a pre-Angkor Cambodian deity head.

COUNTERBALANCE

The difference between interior designs by architects and those by interior designers—at least so most architects claim—is that the former are more interested in space and the manipulation of spatial volumes. Interior designers, they say, are more interested in surface effects. With their restyling of a Park Avenue apartment, the New York interior design team of Bray-Schaible has combined the two emphases. The space is a two-story maisonette in a grand old Manhattan building, and the owners felt that separate formal rooms were not right for their way of living. As Robert Bray explains: "The residents are open, casual and well traveled."

Robert Bray and Michael Schaible began by opening up the spaces on the lower floor and taking down the walls between living and dining rooms, entrance hall and stairs. They left only the mahogany-paneled library and the kitchen isolated as separate rooms. They also left the ceiling moldings of the original wall locations in order to retain some orientation and to give definition to the direction they took next. That was the inclusion of a series of rooms-within-rooms—the smaller being open to the larger, but still palpable as separate spaces. In the living room, for example, a plaster-walled sofa back encloses the conversation area around the fireplace, yet leaves it as part of the overall living area. It is an L-shaped sofa, essentially, built into a wall and—like a park bench—open to the landscape. It is, as Michael Schaible says, "part of the architecture." The small banquette in one nook is separated from the dining room, at its rear, by a partition that rises into a curved overhead cove, yet it is linked to the dining room by a wide pass-through. It is also linked to the living room—to which it is spatially open—by a ledge of Minnesota Kasota stone, which wraps around the corner and runs to the chimney breast.

The adjacent stairway is the focal point of all these multiple "layering" effects, as the technique is called. There the designers have opened the stairwell to provide an axial vista from the entrance, and have made it into a series of multilayered screens and panels. It is a complex progression of rectilinear and curvilinear forms—plane on plane and layer on layer—that rise vertically to be visible from all areas. The work of Bray-Schaible Design generally has an objectless and industrialized approach, like the work of most of the school of interior designing that is called *minimalist*. "Many times we start by doing things that at first may seem eccentric," Bob Bray explains. Here, they have removed window moldings and baseboards as evidence of their basic method of simplification. But then they went on to draw out the potential of what was already there.

The surface colors of the project show a mellowing of the black and white schemes that many people may associate with the designers. Here, a single light color—in wall paint, window coverings and raw-silk upholstery—is combined with the warm-toned Kasota stone for flooring, ledges and the dining table, along with neutral-hued carpeting and touches of black. These black touches, however, are not used exactly in the minimalist manner. In this context they have a dramatic, almost flamboyant, scale and location. In the living room, for instance, a multifold black screen at the end wall is a stereo speaker system, but it is used as others might locate a multicolored painting or a coromandel screen. This speaker is like a black Op painting by Ad Reinhardt. "Black gives punch, clarity and briskness to a space like this," the designers say. Together with this inventive use of color, the spatial arrangement of rooms-within-rooms is a refreshing and intriguing combination of architecture and interior design.

PRECEDING PAGE: *Designers Robert Bray and Michael Schaible boldly renovated a two-story Manhattan apartment, wittily keynoting the Entrance Hall with a window-like cutout and a tall plaster column topped by a cast-iron capital.* ABOVE: *Within the minimalist design of the Living Room, several environments coexist. A low plaster wall defines the space while serving as a sofa back for an L-shaped seating arrangement. Beyond, embraced by the curving wall, a wicker chair appoints a reading nook. The small centaur statue is by Colin Webster Watson.*

ABOVE: *In the Living Room, a Dennis Anderson oil and a delicately proportioned Giacometti bronze enhance a ledge extending into the snug room-within-a-room.* FOLLOWING PAGES: *Ellsworth Kelly lithographs, displayed on sloped panels beneath the windows, establish the aesthetic context in the Living Room. Dark-toned stereo speaker screens in the background suggest a contemporary artwork.*

OPPOSITE: *Ingenious spatial solutions include, in the Dining Room, a curving partition—the back of the living room alcove—penetrated by a horizontal cutout. Wicker chairs and a round stone table restate the curvilinear emphasis.* ABOVE: *Carpet-covered walls lend the warmth of a cocoon to the Master Bedroom. Small sculptures by John Storrs, left, and Jacques Lipchitz, right, inject dark drama.*

HARMONY ACHIEVED

Incomparable art has its own life, and such art makes demands on its viewers and the space it inhabits. The passion that goes into the making of a masterwork, and the imagination expressed through its technique, require a suitable place in which to be seen and felt. It is not an easy task to design rooms that neither clash with fine art nor disappear under its force. When Mr. and Mrs. B. Gerald Cantor, owners and caretakers of one of the world's most extensive private collections of Rodin, decided they needed a home in Los Angeles, they asked designer Bebe Winkler to create an appropriate residence and to select for it pieces from their collection.

Bebe Winkler had designed the Cantors' home in New York and therefore had had experience with their superlative Rodins and their paintings. In New York the Cantor apartment had quite literally been designed around the art, and the designer knew what pieces would be used and where every work would be displayed. In Los Angeles, however, neither Bebe Winkler nor Mrs. Cantor knew exactly which works of art would be in the penthouse until the project was completed at last, in its entirety. It was an unusual situation. The Cantors chose their penthouse apartment before the building was completed. Elliot Saltzman, their New York architect, designed the layout of it on paper; he never came to Los Angeles—and neither did the interior designer, until it was time for the installation. She had everything made in New York and delivered to Los Angeles. She recalls that time with some amazement: "I was working in quarter-inch scale for about six months, and when I finally saw the penthouse apartment I couldn't believe how large it was."

However, for Mr. and Mrs. Cantor, Los Angeles was meant to be different. For some people from Manhattan the "country" is Connecticut or the Hamptons; for the Cantors, going to the "country" is going to Los Angeles. The city serves both as a place to carry on business and for relaxation. "When we are in Los Angeles," says Mrs. Cantor, "we entertain for as many as we can seat in the dining room, which is six. Bebe Winkler treated our home to a lot of color, ranging from delicate blue-greens to daring reds." Important paintings, the designer feels, look better against the right strong colors, and she knows how to use color, both to soothe and stimulate. Set against the wrong hues, the largest Rodins might well have dwarfed everything. Instead, the relationship between color and art is so adroitly handled that the enormous Rodin dominating the living room is perceived as the intellectual and emotional source from which everything else emanates.

In the far corner of the living room three more sculptures are displayed together like a heroic family. There are two Rodins—the *Nude Study for Balzac* and *The Cathedral*—and a Georg Kolbe. The Rodins are pure energy cast in bronze, while the paintings on the wall are lyrical unities of light and color. Accessorizing a room occupied by great art is difficult, and Bebe Winkler chose to include the Oriental porcelains that Mrs. Cantor enjoys collecting. "Many accessories do not mix with sculptures and paintings," says the designer. "Porcelains seem to, and the simpler the better." A conscientious designer can make all the elements of a project work as a harmonious whole, and one room must respond to the next. When a designer is also entrusted with providing surroundings for some very exciting and important artworks, the challenges are even more compelling than usual. The Cantors were fortunate to have a designer as obviously sensitive to art as Bebe Winkler, and together they have achieved a "country" home that is completely functional.

The compelling presence of art guided Bebe Winkler's design for Mr. and Mrs. B. Gerald Cantor's penthouse apartment in Los Angeles. PRECEDING PAGE: A monumental bronze by Rodin entitled The Shade stands in the Living Room.

RIGHT: *Variations on a single hue create a harmonious background in the Living Room. A Georg Kolbe standing female figure is lithe foil for Rodin's* Nude Study for Balzac *and upraised bronze hands. The painting is by Georges d'Espagnat.* BELOW: *De la Fresnaye's* Eve *evokes archetypal serenity in the Living Room. Paintings are by Robert Delaunay (left) and Paul Sérusier.*

RIGHT: Nicki, *a standing bronze by Enzo Plazzotta, lends supple grace in the Master Bedroom. A 1930s influence distinguishes the streamlined lacquered desk, and the draperies and wallcovering infuse the room with the ambience of a garden. Georg Kolbe's lissome bronze,* Sitzendes Mädchen, *occupies a sparkling mirrored niche; his* Kniende *rests on a bedside table.* BELOW: *A small Rodin bronze,* Three Faunesses, *gives energetic form to motion.*

PAST THE MOON GATE

The resident said, "You can go ahead and do what you think I want." Not quite the same as carte blanche, this was a case of talent recognizing talent—and challenging it. In such a way fashion designer Choey Fong asked Anthony Machado to design her Los Angeles apartment, after seeing photographs of Mr. Machado's own San Francisco residence. As Mr. Machado relates, Miss Fong called him and said, "This is the look I want." The interior designer continues: "We met and hit it off right away. She had a whole list of things she wanted—including a throne—but her first stipulation was 'I don't want anything that relates at all to reality.' "

For a venturesome young designer this was a splendid inducement. The list of necessities required by the owner included little in the way of chill reality, and a great deal in the way of the ethereal. What Miss Fong was seeking in her new apartment was, quite simply, serenity—and also fantasy. She envisioned a milieu conducive to her own design work, a place for meditation and inward development. The spaces had to be generalized enough for large groups but particularized for intimate entertaining. It was to be an entirely personal retreat, and yet not static—a place capable of mercurial changes in response to the owner's own flights of imagination.

So, out of a compact condominium residence, Tony Machado created a world whose precise dimensions are beside the point. Essentially, he provided mystery, a setting both glamorous and spare, a tranquil sort of fantasy. Two master stratagems create the striking mood. The first of these is the circular moon gate, finished in high-gloss lacquer and inlaid with brass, that separates the living and bedroom areas. The open arch is both focal point and tangible token of a deliberately created mood of Oriental composure. The other telling element is the enigmatic four-foot brass shield inlaid in mirror, which is reflected throughout the space, deepening the drama and mystery. So vividly is the mood of this private world realized that even the life-size bronze deer in the living area can be accepted without hesitation as being absolutely appropriate.

The entire apartment is composed of pale colors in various textures—polished travertine wall and decks, lacquered shoji screens, reiterated upholstery fabric. Within a neutral shell, accent colors can come and go, and the setting was designed so that Miss Fong could remain in complete control of the finished result. Thus, arriving visitors are invited to slip into robes and slippers. No alien colors or silhouettes are permitted to distract. "Yet, if Miss Fong is in the mood for red," says Mr. Machado, "a set of Chinese red pillows is brought out, along with red flowers, and there might be red robes for the guests. Just these few touches, reflected and refracted endlessly in the mirrored walls, transform the space."

Concealed lighting plays an important part in Miss Fong's apartment. As one of the more functional elements in her list of requirements, the apparel designer wanted a place where she could conduct fashion shows, or that could serve as a setting for performances of the dance, and even for Chinese puppet shows. The moon gate, the mirrors and the flexible lighting provide endless possibilities for drama. To Tony Machado, the spaces he created for Miss Fong suggest his design direction: "a paring away, a return to purity of design." His aim is to find the essence of a particular time or place—as he has done in Miss Fong's apartment, with its Far Eastern aspects—and out of it "to produce an illusion of the total re-creation of an era." Levels of perception are what this apartment is all about. The result is reality, created entirely out of sheer illusion.

PRECEDING PAGE: *Anthony Machado transformed fashion designer Choey Fong's condominium apartment, in Los Angeles, into a tranquil haven.*

ABOVE: *A Chinese moon gate with pale lacquered finish detailed in brass connects the Living Room and bedroom. A scroll table displaying a single Japanese candlestick stands before the custom-designed sofa; behind, an inlaid brass shield subtly punctuates the mirrored wall.*

ABOVE AND FOLLOWING PAGES: *Two life-size bronze deer add to the fantasy of the setting. In the Living Room, the rounded contours of the furniture play gently against the geometric lines of shoji screens. Deft groupings of candles on the terrace echo the refrain of a glittering cityscape.*

ABOVE: *A corner of the Living Room used for dining blends with the quiet, ethereal mood. A glass-topped table with pedestal base is appointed with gracefully sculpted lacquered chairs adapted from a dignified Japanese model.* OPPOSITE: *An arched acrylic centerpiece ornaments the table, accompanied by large black glass plates.*

THE URBAN IMAGE

"Unlike some apartments that could be located in Dallas or Chicago, the residents and I wanted this one to personify New York urban life—sophisticated, functional, with no frills," interior designer Robert Metzger says, as he views the Manhattan panorama stretching into the distance. "I loved doing the apartment since it provided me with a definite change of pace. You see, I think it is death for a designer to be associated with only one look. This is a contemporary apartment, with a mixture of textures, as opposed to my past work, which has been a mixture of objects and antiques. I'm going through a period of growth—a slow but careful and constant metamorphosis. And, speaking of metamorphosis, this apartment went through some drastic changes." The interior space, under the direction of Milton Klein & Associates, was rebuilt, including refreshed architectural detailing and lighting techniques.

"In this project I learned the 'less is more' principle to its fullest extent," continues Mr. Metzger. "There are no fillers in this apartment simply for the sake of beauty alone. I am hired to edit and interpret my clients' needs, and I always strive to maintain a state of cooperation during the installation and after all the work is finally finished. You see, what my work really deals with is people's lives, and in this case it was a domestic unit for which I worked out a solution that was dramatic and in good taste. The resident relies on professionals. She knows her limitations and her capabilities. Though she allowed me great freedom, we discussed everything. I feel that if a client will not listen to a designer, then he or she has no right to engage one. The relationship between designer and client is a sort of marriage."

The concept of marriage in design is exemplified by Mr. Metzger in the living area, where the interplay of fabrics is harmonious—upholstered woolen walls serving as a backdrop for the silk, satin, cotton and velvet of the furnishings. Further counterpoints can be seen in the eighteenth-century chinoiserie chairs and the Frankenthaler painting, which blend well with an extensive collection of Japanese, Chinese and Korean artifacts. The placement of these objects divides space and delineates limits, but it in no way inhibits or curtails the openness maintained throughout the entire apartment.

The library area is an extension of the living area, combining the contemporary color schemes of both rooms. The sectional sofa provides additional seating for those waiting to play at the games table, which is illuminated from all sides. "I'm always very aware of lighting," says the designer. "It has to do with vanity, I suppose. Without proper lighting, neither my design nor the clients will look their best. But you can't be a maven on everything. If I can't do something, I call a professional *immediately*! That's part of the reason this 'marriage' worked. I *insist* on perfection; I *insist* on maintaining my standards."

The dining room, comfortably seating from four to sixteen, perhaps best illustrates Mr. Metzger's insistence on care. The walls and recessed, hinged folding doors with innumerable layers of hand-mottled lacquer seem to form a jewel, shining from the inner brilliance of brass, stainless steel, parchment and ivory combined in the expandable dining tables. "I love creating visual mysteries," says the designer. Musing over the finished project, Mr. Metzger goes on, "It was a year of my life, and the end result is so satisfying I'd do it again. For me, everything is perfect—as perfect as humanly possible. The problem with people today is that they have learned—actually been conditioned—to accept less. We seem to have forgotten that there can be such a thing as perfection. It is entirely possible."

Designer Robert Metzger's assured use of color and texture endows a Manhattan apartment with urbane vitality. PRECEDING PAGE AND RIGHT: *In the Living Room, walls and sofas in a neutral hue provide a subtle foil for large contemporary artworks. The shaped painting is by Kenneth Noland, the tall metal sculpture by Joel Perlman, and the large rectangular canvas by Helen Frankenthaler. A sleek multitiered table serves as the unifying focal point, its transparent layers bearing a cinnabar box and a triple-tube vase. Distinctive K'ang-hsi armchairs complement the delicate motifs of an antique Chinese rug.*

RIGHT AND OPPOSITE: *Recessed strip lighting and reflective surfaces establish a sophisticated mood in the Dining Room and the adjoining Foyer. A cinnabar table screen atop a sandalwood altar table—both 18th-century Chinese—mingle with 19th-century blue and white porcelain to instill Oriental grace. Shimmering with mystery, lustrous lacquered panels backdrop small tables that permit dining flexibility.*

High contrast and controlled lighting
create a beguiling chiaroscuro effect in
an informal Bedroom. A diagonal
emphasis prevails, introduced by an
angled wall that forms a study nook
and conceals storage. Striped carpeting
restates both the diagonal thrust and
the color contrast of walls and ceiling.
The painting is by Robert Goodnough.

The Master Bedroom is a roseate
bower with painted silk wall upholstery
and lively primrose fabric. Porcelain
objects displayed in recessed shelves
accentuate the color scheme, while a
simplified window treatment gives full
play to the urban panorama. The Near
Eastern mirror, ornately adorned with
mother-of-pearl, is 19th-century.

PROGRESSIONS

Architects who are asked to rework conventional apartments in old Park Avenue buildings usually do so by attacking the floor plan. They make their mark by altering the apartment spatially, changing shapes and opening up rooms. It is a method of redesign that often yields attractive living spaces, but rarely permits the architect much leeway in expressing any theoretical ideas. Piero Sartogo, an Italian architect now practicing in New York, has managed to create an exception to the trend. In renovating a full floor of an old and relatively unexceptional Park Avenue building, he was able to explore certain ideas concerning the nature of architectural experience.

The architect, working with his colleague, Michael Schwarting, chose to challenge conventional notions of what rooms are, what the relationship of rooms to each other is, and what luxury is. The basic layout of the apartment has not been altered, but Mr. Sartogo moved some doors, and eliminated others, to create a different organization that sharply regulates the sequence in which rooms are experienced. The idea of sequence is the crucial one here. Piero Sartogo's rearrangement of doors made it possible to have only one progression of movement through the public rooms of the apartment. Instead of moving from the entrance hall to any of the rooms, it is necessary to go from there to the library, from the library to the living room, from the living room to the dining room. These rooms together are seen as elements in a progression, and every aspect of their design is intended to express this notion. Mr. Sartogo worked with Italian artist Giulio Paolini to create a scheme that would tie the four rooms together and be, in itself, a work of conceptual art. The sequence design has two basic elements: an aluminum grid on the terrazzo floor and on the plaster ceiling, which alters in size as one moves from the entrance hall toward the dining room; and a series of columns, designed by Paolini, that vary in number and dimension as the sequence progresses.

The sequence begins in the entrance hall, where four columns are set, freestanding. The locations of the columns are marked on the floor by the grid of aluminum strips, which in this room are 1/8 inch wide. Each column begins with a Doric base, but a few feet up, instead of a capital, there is a narrower version of the same Doric base set on top of the original column. A still narrower version is set on top of that, and so on, until the column disappears as a sliver into the ceiling. In the library, the themes established in the entrance hall begin their variations. The grid in the floor expands to strips 1/4 inch wide, and the columns grow bigger and fewer. There are two columns here, instead of four, and the bases have expanded so that there is not room for the theme of little column atop bigger one to be repeated as often as before. In the living room is a still larger grid of one-inch aluminum strips, and one enormous column. The dining room, the final room of the sequence, has no column at all. By now, if the expansion were to have continued at its present rate, the room would have had just one huge column, like a sequoia tree trunk, in the middle. The grid moves up to a two-inch width at the end of this room, hitting the far wall—a gesture intended to emphasize that the grid is a work of conceptual art.

The aura of the apartment, for all its insistence on being a theoretical exercise, is that of classicism. It is startlingly modern, but one feels the sensibility of a classical Italian palazzo informing and stimulating the architect's ideas. This feeling of classicism in the midst of experimentation is perhaps the finest quality—and it is the most subtle of all the contradictions Piero Sartogo has chosen to explore here.

Exploring ideas about space and sequence, architect Piero Sartogo and his associate, Michael Schwarting, transformed a Park Avenue apartment, in Manhattan, into a conceptual yet livable environment. PRECEDING PAGE: *Jannis Kounellis's construction with oil lamp and Cy Twombly's* Arcadia *distinguish the Living Room.* ABOVE: *In the Library, telescope-like columns—a design element connecting adjacent rooms—and terrazzo flooring recall a classical Italian palazzo.*

TOP: *Fortunato Depero's 1907 cyclist evokes the early days of Italian Futurism.* ABOVE: *In the main rooms, doors—complete with moldings and baseboards—are sections of wall cut away, mounted on hinges and set into the resultant openings. Inspired by this approach, an artwork by Joseph Kosuth includes a photograph of a door, an actual door and, at the right, a definition of a door.*

115

PARTIC. DEI CONIUGI ARNOLFINI

PRECEDING PAGES: *In the Dining Room, a surprisingly traditional Sheraton table and Chippendale-style chairs dominate the gallerylike space. Joining Kosuth's Door are works by Italian Pop artists Mario Schifano (left) and Tano Festa (right).*

118

A spare geometry defines the mood in the Master
Bedroom and adjoining bath, with their butcher-
block walls and flooring, and neutral carpeting.
A sense of movement is introduced in a large
canvas by Mario Schifano. Behind the painting,
doors slide out of view.

RICHES OF THE EAST

In the brief cool spell that residents of Hong Kong rather fancifully call winter, a log fire burns invitingly in the large, high-ceilinged living room of Mr. and Mrs. Adrian Zecha's home. Turning from the leaping flames to the large window, their many guests who are new to Hong Kong can hardly refrain from a gasp of astonishment at the incredible view of the city and the harbor. The residence is a duplex apartment with a roof terrace, one of only sixteen in a small block high up on The Peak, the soaring little mountain that springs from the harbor waters and the stalagmites of city blocks far below. "We like to live in an amiable place," says Adrian Zecha. "My wife and I both dislike a 'decorator' look. We are serious collectors, and we love the things we have. We are always trying to refine the collection down to the major and most attractive pieces."

When they found the apartment it was not yet complete, and it was the large, empty spaces that attracted them both—the possibilities, rather than the reality. "We looked for an interior designer and turned to a young and extremely talented Filipino named Jun Alday. He has a marvelous clean sort of taste, and this exactly suited us. We looked long and hard at the spaces and then quite literally placed the works of art we wanted in the positions we wanted them to occupy—to scale, on the plans. The final design was done entirely around the collections." The obvious danger in this approach is the "museum look," happily avoided in the unstudied living and dining areas. The entrance hall strikes a warmly wood-paneled note. A Ceylonese-Dutch sofa occupies a space especially designed for it under a large Udaipur Indian painting on cloth, of the eternally joyous lover-god Krishna. "In acquiring works of art," says Adrian Zecha, "we've always first considered what we feel to be the major cultural contribu-

tion of each country to the art heritage of the East. So we chose Indian wood sculpture rather than Chinese, and Indian stone sculpture and that of the Khmer—and, of course, Indian miniature and also Tantric painting." The dining room is simple almost to the point of bareness. A round Jehol table that displays the richness of Chinese marquetry at its best is at center stage. A Korean palace screen is on one wall, while another wall displays a Tantric Indian painting. A huge wooden horse's head, part of an ancient chariot of the gods used ceremonially in East and South India, graces the window alcove.

When not entertaining, the Zechas live upstairs. The long room there, running the whole width of the apartment, is both sleeping and living area, divisible by retractable screens. An alcove off the main area conceals the brass four-poster bed. While the character of the downstairs rooms is certainly neither cold nor formal, the quarters above have a kind of intimacy that belongs with family life.

Adrian Zecha has one of the rare and definitive Annamese porcelain collections in private hands—each piece the end product not only of the special skills of the ancient potters of North Vietnam but also the result of his own persistence in upgrading the collection. Indeed, Jun Alday had a small museum constructed to house it. Here also are selected examples of Chinese Export ware, once shipped all over Asia and far beyond. The "museum" is one area not seen by most visitors. In Asia, collectors tend to show their treasures only to those who have some knowledge of the subject. Even then, only a part of the collection is displayed at any one time. Ultimately, the Zechas say, they want to simplify living, and not to be prisoners of their possessions. In the arrangement of their apartment in Hong Kong, they have almost achieved that commendable goal.

Mr. and Mrs. Adrian Zecha's apartment in Hong Kong was designed by Jun Alday to highlight a collection of Oriental treasures. PRECEDING PAGE: *Illumination heightens the delicacy of Chinese porcelain objects within a symmetrical Living Room arrangement.* RIGHT: *In concert, the owners and designer created a special setting for each cherished object, as in the Entrance Hall, where a niche frames a Dutch cabinet from Ceylon. The wooden figures are Indian.*

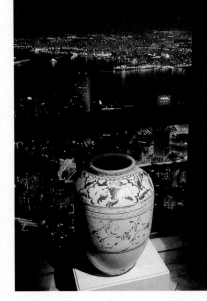

TOP AND TOP RIGHT: *A trove of rare Annamese porcelain containers includes a trio of graceful vessels.* ABOVE AND ABOVE RIGHT: *A haniwa horse head and a Sung Dynasty jar bridge a millennium, against the modern spectacle of Hong Kong's harbor.*

Honed, like the entire collection, to essential simplicity, the Dining Room is appointed with a Chinese table and elegant Ming Dynasty chairs. From India, a wooden horse head, in front of the bay window, and a standing horse figure provide subtle cultural contrast to a Korean screen.

A Khmer stone sculpture and a Ming
Dynasty painting adorn the upstairs
Master Bedroom. The room also
functions as a comfortable study.

Harboring a gleaming brass bed, a secluded alcove of the Master Bedroom conveys a serene feeling of Eastern tranquility. The portrait is by Bravo.

THE IMPACT OF ART

Every now and then, one element of design is singled out to be the principal theme of a room or series of rooms, and there will be a fugal play on color, shape or style. However, interiors composed around the manipulation of scale are something special and rather less definable. In a New York apartment that Angelo Donghia designed, scale is demonstrated explosively and wondrously. The most prominent and powerful effect comes from a collection of paintings by the Colombian artist Fernando Botero—perhaps the most extensive assemblage of the artist's work anywhere—although the residents also display fine works by Victor Vasarely, Francis Bacon and Picasso from their collection. Interior designer Donghia has shrewdly recognized the merits of the Botero paintings and their relationship to the apartment design. "They're so big and strong, and they occupy so much wall space," he explains. Botero's work definitely suggests the inherent juxtaposition of human scale and superscale, although always within the context of the paintings themselves. It is a mannered, and Mannerist, vision of the known order of human size. And in the apartment orchestrated for them by Mr. Donghia, Botero's paintings produce a trembling, a virtual earthquake, between the scale of the images, the scale of the rooms and the view that lies beyond them.

Angelo Donghia brought to this interior design not only his acumen and decision-making skills, but also a personal style that is varied and eclectic. He started by making the right first decisions—accepting immediately that the prospect over Central Park to the skyscraper skyline was easily the most spectacular physical feature of the apartment, and that everything should be subservient to the view and the paintings. He knew that all of this had to be capitalized on, in spite of the contradictory requirements of the spatial context. He had to open up the view without damaging the paintings with daylight or protecting them by concealing the cityscape. Although the apartment is relatively large, the rooms as such are somewhat small. Still, they have ceilings that, at nine feet, are rather higher than those of the usual Manhattan apartment. So Mr. Donghia determined to expand the apparent room size by treating all the principal spaces—entrance hall, living room and dining room—as a single entity, with an overall muted and monochromatic color scheme.

Almost as an aside, Mr. Donghia speaks of tidying up the architectural envelope—squaring up the windows with consistent valance heights, built-out sills and surrounding walls. And he points out something that might otherwise be overlooked: Although the windows themselves are not unattractive, the view has been expanded by mirroring the reveals alongside them, and the only window coverings are slim venetian blinds. He also widened the doorways in the principal rooms to increase the flow, and he installed sliding doors. Then, in order to give the rooms a certain "architectural embellishment," as he calls it, the designer added a polished brass molding at the ceiling line. This gives a flavor of French Modern design—no surprise, as Mr. Donghia recalls his favorite inspiration, the work of Jean-Michel Frank.

Within this newly ordered background, as if to reiterate the scale and the rhythm of forms that appear in the Botero paintings, the interior designer chose furniture that is squat, plump, short—but quite large. "It is a strange combination, to put pictures of this size in so small a room," Mr. Donghia observes. "The rooms are scaled for people, while the paintings are scaled to a colossus." With consummate artistry and insight, the designer has turned this Mannerist scale play into a deft design motif.

128

A skillful orchestration of scale, form, view—and artworks—characterizes Angelo Donghia's design for a Manhattan apartment. PRECEDING PAGE: *A large canvas by Botero dominates the Entrance Hall.* RIGHT: *The Manhattan skyline holds sway in the Living Room, serving as a stunning backdrop for commodious seating. Brass ceiling moldings edge walls covered in silk. A play of scale occurs between the figures in the Botero painting itself.*

OPPOSITE: *An 18th-century chandelier instills sparkle in the Dining Room. Here, and in the living room beyond, are paintings and a sculpture by Botero depicting fruit.* ABOVE: *An intense Francis Bacon triptych is displayed in the Library.*

Modulations of the earth-toned motif that unifies the residence extend to the Master Bedroom, a shadowy, intimate nest with soft upholstery and a clutch of pillows. The suede patchwork wall-covering echoes the geometry of the patterned cotton fabric used extensively. Rendered in sanguine on canvas, a reclining nude exhibits the embonpoint that distinguishes Botero's figures; a Botero pastel graces the wall above the bed with sophisticated naiveté. Evoking 1920s Art Nouveau, an opalescent glass vessel gleams at bedside.

PRESENT AND PAST IN MADRID

The European interior designer frequently has at his disposal far more intriguing and imaginative material with which to work than does his American counterpart. The difference, of course, has nothing to do with talent or skill, but rather with the obvious truth that a European designer can take advantage of the architecture and variety of far older civilizations. The heritage of these older civilizations is especially striking when it is combined with the most contemporary concepts in twentieth-century interior design, a felicitous combination that the Spanish design team of Román Arango and Pin Morales have so fully achieved in their own home.

The large apartment is situated in one of the loveliest sections of Madrid, on the Plaza de Oriente opposite the royal palace. The proportions were more than generous, since, with the exception of the eighteenth-century palace, all the buildings on the plaza were built during the nineteenth century, when space was not at a premium and not the luxury it has become in contemporary times. Indeed, the Plaza de Oriente is one of the most appealing of those enchanted locales in Madrid. Like other apartments there, the apartment Señor Arango and Señor Morales occupy looks over a large expanse of garden in the center of which is an equestrian statue of Philip IV of Spain, a splendid work by the Florentine sculptor Pietro Tacca. The orientation of their apartment, however, allows it not only to overlook the garden but to face the majestic Palacio Real itself as well. Both designers feel it is "one of the most impressive buildings in Europe," and they are fortunate that their view extends beyond the palace, across the green expanse of the Casa de Campo, to the snow-capped Sierra de Guadarrama. Indeed, these very mountains figure in many a painting executed by the great Velázquez himself. "To be

sure, we are prejudiced," the designers explain, "but there can't be many locations like this in the world."

They may very well be right, and this superb setting has given them every opportunity to put into practice their desire to harmonize the old and the new. However forward-looking they may be, they would never deny beauty from the past, and the interiors they have created for their apartment confirm this. Facing west, the apartment is particularly impressive at the close of the day. Then the orange and purple rays of the setting sun are captured in the mirrored entrance hall. The effect is much like a painting, and it is indeed a prelude to the designers' approach to the rest of the residence.

For all the elaborations of the plaza outside and the building in which it is located, the apartment is perhaps most notable for its simplicity of line. A pure and linear quality is seen in the furniture and in the fabrics used. Often these will depict representations of lilies, and they are similar to other fabrics the designers create exclusively for their clients. The simplicity of line is deceptive, however, since both Señor Arango and Señor Morales delight in the occasional surprise of a Baroque or unusual object, like the sixteenth-century statuette attributed to El Greco, which they found in a village near Toledo. Surprise, too, comes in the rearrangement the two are always making of flowers or interesting stones or small objects. "Without sounding pretentious," says Román Arango, "we consider it the duty of a designer to change and experiment constantly. Besides, we *like* to do it." The result of their experimentation is an appealing beauty and a sensitive mixture of the new and the old. It is said that Beauty often rewards her admirers, and this apartment in the Plaza de Oriente can surely be interpreted as a fitting reward for Román Arango and Pin Morales.

Designers Román Arango and Pin Morales
infused their Madrid home with the refinement
of their shared aesthetic. PRECEDING PAGES: *In the
Living Room, etchings by Rossini are exhibited
beyond a row of columns painted with calli-
graphic designs by Sr. Morales. Other artworks
in the room are by the two designers, individually
as well as in collaboration.* ABOVE: *In the Studio,
works of art by friends of the designers line the
walls, surrounding a curious object from antiquity,
an Egyptian dynastic canopic jar.* RIGHT: *An
arrangement of Phoenician and Iberian-Roman
pottery expresses an archaeological leitmotiv.
The paleontologic fantasy is by José Fernandez.*

In the Hall, mirrored surfaces create spatial illusion with an infinity of reflections. A mirrored pyramid hangs from the ceiling, suspending an iron chandelier above an unadorned pine table. A single chair and a pair of astrolabes heighten the contrast between the simple, fundamental objects and their complex, radiantly modern setting.

OPPOSITE: *In the Dressing Room, a chest displays a sculpture by the two designers; the painting is by La Huerta. Mirrored columns flank the arrangement.* ABOVE: *Focal point of the simplified Bed/Sitting Room is a Spanish Renaissance carved and polychromed wood figure of St. John; the early-17th-century work has been attributed to El Greco. The pointillist painting is by Sr. Arango.*

143

FIELD OF VISION

"Spatial ambiguities" is the description John Saladino gives to those stylistic devices that allow him to conquer the inhuman rigors of steel-and-glass highrise interiors. "To overcome the tyranny of a lot of little six-planed boxes," he explains, "you must aim for a sort of elegant alienation, where volumes and boundaries remain somewhat indeterminate. Once you fully determine a space, it seems to me destroyed, and I become bored. I try to create something of the quality that is found in Japanese houses—fluidity and ambiguity working together." An apartment at the United Nations Plaza, in New York, demonstrates the aptness of the architect-interior designer's theories. He began with a space that was generous in size and that had a remarkable view of the East River. Nevertheless, it was a traditional duplex apartment with formal floor plan and nine-foot ceilings. From this beginning Mr. Saladino created a fluid interior where rooms now blend with each other in a gentle flow and interchange.

The project began with massive demolition and reconstruction. Dividing walls fell to leave support columns isolated; a steel stringer was left exposed to allow the staircase to "float"; the fireplace was wrapped in stainless steel and acts as a free agent in space, "zoning" the dining room from the living room. The volume of auxiliary spaces—closets, a stereo center and service core—was cut to make the nine-foot ceilings seem higher by contrast. "I'm a minimalist in terms of what I feel architecturally," says the designer, "and I hold off my 'sense of closure' a lot longer than other minimalists." Throughout the apartment, passages from one room to another are announced more by changes in visual dynamics than by enclosing physical limits. It is a technique that has become, in many ways, a hallmark of Mr. Saladino's work in interior design.

The interiors are made eventful not only by means of subtle architectural plays, but also by the furnishings themselves. The living room is divided into two areas by an angled sofa arrangement—one focused on the fireplace, the other on the spectacular view. The placement at once animates and relaxes the interior. "Furniture at ninety-degree angles doesn't necessarily have to do with people, it has to do with the vignettes of interior design," says John Saladino. "But I am more interested in the humanity of place." Where his architecture may justly be termed "hard edge," his use of color is softening and even nostalgic. There is a unifying "biscuit" tone throughout the interior, with soft-hued accents—"an interplay of elusive, subtle colors," in his words, "which gives sensual contrast to the powerful shapes and large feeling of space. With the exception of the den, which is in mahogany, I have used the kind of shades you might well find in Oriental watercolors or Pre-Raphaelite paintings."

Nowhere in the New York duplex apartment are there any of the unlivable "design statements" popular with some designers. There are personal and obvious romantic choices—like the faded Khotan rugs. The unselfconscious, easy mixture of materials coexists comfortably with the happy contrast of simplicity and lyrical color. The conscious and express desire is not to let interior space be fully understood, not to be straightforward and definite, not to overwhelm with any strongly imposed sense of specific place. At the same time, this environment exudes an unabashed sense of urbanity and luxury that Mr. Saladino maintains "couldn't be imagined except in New York, Milan or perhaps Rio." It is an interior landscape with both architectural integrity and spatial ambiguity. It is, on the other hand, also a very human and joyous celebration of living.

*Interior designer John Saladino revitalized a
New York apartment by minimizing closed
areas.* PRECEDING PAGE: *A fireplace partitions the
Living Room from the dining area. The colors in
an antique Khotan rug are echoed in the sofa
upholstery.* ABOVE: *An up-lighted curved volume
replaces a traditional wall in the Living Room.*

The polished stainless-steel fireplace partition
reflects a mirror image of the Dining Area.
Beyond, an interplay of subtle tones, enhanced by
discreet lighting, encourages visual continuity
between rooms. The original boxlike confines of
the apartment were overcome by establishing
somewhat indeterminate boundaries and volumes.

ABOVE: *A partially mirrored wall doubles the spaciousness of a spare, uncluttered Bedroom, where a contoured desk, bed and cabinet form a crisp unit. Bright colors in a hard-edge painting, seen in reflection, accent the otherwise pale tones of the room. A wooden chaise longue is drawn close to the window—and the view. The ribbed floor covering offers subtle linear contrast to the rounded shapes of the furniture.*

TOP: *A curved closet provides a barrier between a bedroom and an upstairs Corridor. Dramatic lighting casts a glint on the stainless-steel railing of the stairway. Mirrors heighten the glimmer.*
ABOVE AND FOLLOWING PAGES: *Glass panels near the ceiling appear to enlarge the Master Bedroom and diminish the sense of enclosure.*

149

CREDITS

WRITERS

The following writers prepared the original *Architectural Digest* articles from which the material in this book has been adapted:

Nigel Cameron

Peter Carlsen

Paula Deitz

Luis Escobar

Jean-Louis Gaillemin

Paul Goldberger

Lois Wagner Green

Elizabeth Lambert

John Loring

Cameron Curtis McKinley

Suzanne Stark Morrow

Carolyn Noren

C. Ray Smith

Gerrold A. Turnbull

All original text adapted by Cameron Curtis McKinley.

All original captions adapted by Kirsten Grimstad.

PHOTOGRAPHERS

Jaime Ardiles-Arce 16–23, 32–39, 66–75, 82–89, 104–111, 112–119, 128–135, 144–151

Elizabeth Heyert 24–31, 48–55

Pascal Hinous 56–65, 76–81

Leland Y. Lee 96–103

Russell MacMasters 40–47

Derry Moore 10–15

Mary E. Nichols 2–9

José Luis Pérez 136–143

Charles S. White 90–95, 120–127

DESIGN

Design Direction:
Philip Kaplan, Executive Graphics Director
Knapp Communications Corporation

Book Design and Production:
Glen Iwasaki
B.T. Miyake Productions

MA